JR. GRAPHIC MONSTER STORIES

THE UNDEAD!

MERCY L

STEVEN ROBERTS

PowerKiDS
press

New York

Published in 2014 by The Rosen Publishing Group, Inc.
29 East 21st Street, New York, NY 10010

First Edition

Editor: Joanne Randolph
Book Design: Planman Technologies
Illustrations: Planman Technologies

Publisher Cataloging Data

Roberts, Steven.
The undead! / by Steven Roberts.
p. cm. — (Jr. graphic monster stories)
Includes index.
ISBN 978-1-4777-6207-3 (library binding) — ISBN 978-1-4777-6208-0 (pbk.) — ISBN 978-1-4777-6209-7 (6-pack)
1. Vampires — Juvenile literature. 2. Zombies — Juvenile literature. I. Roberts, Steven. II. Title.
BF1556.R63 2014
398—d23

Manufactured in the United States of America
CPSIA Compliance Information: Batch # W14PK1: For Further Information contact Rosen Publishing, New York, New York at 1-800-237-9932

Contents

Main Characters

George Brown (ca. 1800s) A farmer from Exeter, Rhode Island, and father of Mercy Brown.

Mary Eliza Brown (ca. 1800s) George Brown's wife and the mother of Mercy Brown.

Mary Olive Brown (1864–1884) George Brown's older daughter.

Mercy Lena Brown (1873–1892) George Brown's younger daughter.

Edwin Brown (?–1884) George Brown's son.

About the Undead

The undead are those who show some signs of life after death. They can be **zombies**, vampires, ghosts, mummies, or other supernatural beings. According to legend, certain undead creatures may arise from the grave to haunt or hurt the living.

The Undead!

"ANOTHER FAMOUS UNDEAD CREATURE IS THE **STRIGOI**, FROM ROMANIA. THESE VAMPIRES WERE THE SOULS OF THE DEAD ARISEN FROM THE GRAVE."

"THIS CREATURE STALKED HUMAN PREY IN ITS SEARCH FOR BLOOD."

"THOSE THOUGHT TO BE VAMPIRES WERE REBURIED FACE DOWN SO THEY WOULD DIG THEMSELVES FURTHER INTO THE EARTH."

THE CREATURE LIVES!

TURN OVER THE CORPSE!

"VILLAGERS DROVE SHARP STAKES INTO THE EARTH ABOVE THE GRAVE. IF THE VAMPIRE DUG ITS WAY OUT, IT WOULD **IMPALE** ITSELF."

"DURING THE 1800S, **TUBERCULOSIS**, A LUNG DISEASE, WAS VERY COMMON. THE DISEASE WAS ALSO CALLED **CONSUMPTION**. THERE WAS NO CURE."

"PEOPLE WITH CONSUMPTION BECAME WEAK AND PALE AND COUGHED FREQUENTLY. THIS COULD SPREAD THE DISEASE TO OTHER PEOPLE."

COUGH!

"CONSUMPTION FIRST STRUCK THE BROWN FAMILY IN 1883 WHEN GEORGE'S WIFE, MARY ELIZA BROWN, BECAME SICK."

MARY, I THOUGHT YOU WERE FEELING BETTER.

COUGH! COUGH!

"SEVEN YEARS LATER, GEORGE'S SON, EDWIN, BECAME SICK."

DRINK SOME TEA, SON. IT WILL MAKE YOU FEEL BETTER.

"GEORGE THOUGHT THE MINERAL WATERS OF A COLORADO **SPA** MIGHT HELP CURE EDWIN, SO HE SENT HIM THERE."

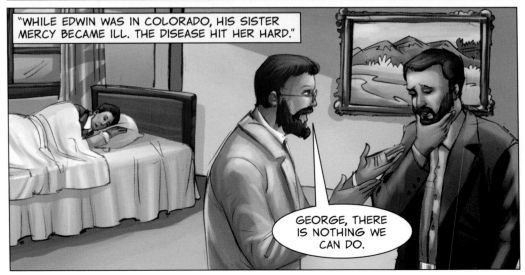

"WHILE EDWIN WAS IN COLORADO, HIS SISTER MERCY BECAME ILL. THE DISEASE HIT HER HARD."

GEORGE, THERE IS NOTHING WE CAN DO.

"MERCY BROWN WAS BURIED IN JANUARY 1892."

"EDWIN RETURNED HOME FROM COLORADO. HIS CONDITION QUICKLY GREW WORSE."

I CANNOT LOSE MY SON!

"ONE OF THE VILLAGERS SAID HE SAW MERCY BROWN WANDERING THE FIELDS NEAR HER HOME."

19

SHE BLEEDS!
VAMPIRE!

"THE VILLAGERS TOOK THIS AS PROOF THAT MERCY WAS CAUSING EDWIN'S ILLNESS."
SHE IS KILLING EDWIN! SHE COULD ATTACK US NEXT!
THERE IS ONLY ONE WAY TO CURE EDWIN AND KILL THE VAMPIRE!

"THE VILLAGERS REMOVED MERCY'S HEART."
YOU MUST BURN THE HEART TO ASHES!

More Undead Stories

- **The Strigoi**
  The Romanian strigoi is the forerunner of the vampire. There are many types of strigoi. One type of strigoi comes back from the dead and returns to its family. It carries on as if nothing has happened while sucking the life out of the other family members until they die.

- **The Strange Tale of Clairvius Narcisse**
  Clairvius Narcisse is the most convincing case of a real zombie. He was thought to have died in 1962 in Haiti. However, he reappeared in 1980. According to Narcisse, his problems began when he got into an argument with his brother over land. His brother hired a bokor, or witch doctor, to drug him and had him buried alive. He was dug up and forced to work as a slave with other zombies. He escaped after two years of enslavement and then roamed the countryside for years hiding from his brother.

- **Unusual Rituals**
  In many cultures, there are rituals that are meant to keep the dead from coming back to life. Tombstones are made of heavy stone to weigh down spirits who might be trying to get out of the grave. The Saxons, a group that lived in England in the Middle Ages, would cut off the feet of the dead so they could not walk fast if they came back to life. In other cultures, people would cut off the head of a corpse. That way if it came back to life, it would be too busy looking for its head to bother the living.

- **Mary Shelley's *Frankenstein***
  An important work in horror literature involving the undead is *Frankenstein; or, the Modern Prometheus,* by Mary Shelley. This novel, published in 1818, tells the story of a scientist named Victor Frankenstein who gives life to a deformed creature who finds it impossible to become a member of human society.

Glossary

bokor (boh-KOR) Someone who feeds someone else a drug to make him or her a slave.

consumption (kun-SUMP-shun) A lung disease, also called tuberculosis, that caused the body to waste away.

draugur (DROW-gur) An undead Viking who lived in his tomb.

impale (im-PAYL) To pierce with something pointed.

spa (SPAH) A resort with mineral springs.

strigoi (STREE-goy) The souls of the dead who had risen from the grave.

suffocate (SUH-fuh-kayt) To die from lack of air.

tuberculosis (too-ber-kyuh-LOH-sis) An illness that affects the lungs.

unearthed (un-ERTHD) Dug up out of the earth.

Viking (VY-king) A member of a group of Scandinavian sailors who attacked the coasts of Europe from the eighth to the tenth centuries.

voodoo (VOO-doo) A religion practiced in Haiti that is based in African religions and the practice of worshipping ancestors.

vrykolakas (VREE-koh-lahk) An undead creature in Greek folklore that harms people.

zombies (ZOM-beez) People who are said to have died and been brought back to life but without a will of their own and unable to speak.

Index

Websites

Due to the changing nature of Internet links, PowerKids Press has developed an online list of websites related to the subject of this book. This site is updated regularly. Please use this link to access the list:

www.powerkidslinks.com/mons/undead